Portrait of
SAN FRANCISCO

Photography by CHUCK HANEY

Text by PETER FISH

RIGHT: Fisherman's Wharf's neon dazzle belies its 19th-century roots as an Italian fishing community, whose sailboats brought in crab and tuna from the waters of San Francisco Bay and the open ocean out past the Golden Gate. While the wharf remains a working fishing port, it's also a major tourist destination, with visitors drawn to attractions like Pier 39 and the Aquarium of the Bay—and to the dozens of seafood restaurants that line the waterfront, among them Alioto's, run by a family prominent in San Francisco politics for generations.

TITLE PAGE: At night, Russian Hill's serpentine Lombard Street glows with taillights, as cars creep down the eight curves that make this the most famously crooked street in the world. (It is not, however, the most crooked street in San Francisco—that honor is usually awarded to Vermont Street, on Potrero Hill.) Behind it, Coit Tower gleams atop neighboring Telegraph Hill. The white concrete tower was built, in 1933, from money donated by eccentric millionaire Lillie Hitchcock Coit, as a tribute to San Francisco's volunteer firemen. Despite the legends, it was not actually designed to resemble a fire hose's nozzle.

FRONT COVER: The iconic, graceful span of the Golden Gate Bridge links San Francisco with Marin County to the north. Opened in 1937, the bridge immediately became a symbol of the City by the Bay.

BACK COVER: The 853-foot spire of the Transamerica Pyramid pierces the San Francisco dusk. Behind it shines the cobalt-lit column of Coit Tower, atop Telegraph Hill, with the waters of San Francisco Bay sweeping north and east past Alcatraz Island to the hills of Marin County.

FRONT FLAP, TOP: A San Francisco icon since it opened in 1898, the Ferry Building commands the city's Embarcadero waterfront. Today the building with its 245-foot clock tower serves as both a commuter hub and the home to an artisan-food-filled marketplace.

FRONT FLAP, BOTTOM: One of San Francisco's signature cable cars rattles up and down the city's hills. The creation of English inventor Andrew Smith Hallidie, the cars began operation in 1873.

ISBN: 978-1-56037-578-4

© 2017 by Farcountry Press
Photography © 2017 by Chuck Haney
Foreword by Chuck Haney
Text by Peter Fish
San Francisco Zoo and Gardens photos, page 39, © 2017 Marianne Hale

For more information about our books, write Farcountry Press, P.O. Box 5630, Helena, MT 59604; call (800) 821-3874; or visit www.farcountrypress.com.

Produced in the United States of America.
Printed in China.

22 21 20 19 18 17   1 2 3 4 5 6

FOREWORD

By Chuck Haney

Maybe you are wondering how a Montana photographer ended up being inspired to shoot images for a coffee-table book on San Francisco? The answer is that I've always had an affinity for the cutting edge counterculture that San Francisco embodies.

Half a lifetime ago, as a young California resident of that rival metropolis to the south, Los Angeles, my friend Billy and I drove a 4-speed 1976 Camaro lugging a U-Haul trailer with all my worldly possessions hundreds of miles out of our

turns onto some insanely steep hills, I almost left my clutch in San Francisco!

After that initial encounter, I always dreamt of returning to San Francisco. But it was only a decade ago that I started to routinely travel to the city. Enticed by cheap airfare and the romantic allure of urban exploration, I found a unique vibe and a spirit in San Francisco that I had not felt or experienced anywhere else. With each subsequent visit, I would walk a bit

way for the sole purpose of seeing San Francisco and driving across the famed Golden Gate Bridge. It's been said that most folks leave their heart in San Francisco. After a few wrong

farther, explore more neighborhoods, and make friends along the way. I was charmed by the clang of cable car bells, enamored by the amazing array of food choices, excited about the diversity of the people I encountered, and exhilarated by the steep grades of the city's famous streets.

As a photographer who is at home on a remote mountain trail or watching a flock of birds, shooting in San Francisco was a stimulating and uplifting experience. Capturing urban settings, where winding streets, Victorian-style architecture, and city lights are the main components of a successful image, has represented a revelation for my career. Cityscapes presented a fresh and delightful challenge to my photographic repertoire.

It has been an interesting time in history to record San Francisco as it goes through changes, both to its landscape and culture. While challenging to keep up with all the alterations, I have enjoyed every step of the journey.

Most days shooting, I have a plan when I head out the door. In San Francisco, my most memorable images occurred when I just took off on foot from my lodging in Russian Hill and discovered things like hidden stairways leading to tiny parks laced with blooming gardens, or quaint narrow streets like Macondray Lane. Wandering around at dawn while most of the city was still asleep was both rewarding and rejuvenating as I blended the peaceful ambient light with the glow of city lights.

While I initially resisted going to tourist-laden venues like Alcatraz, I was pleasantly surprised after wandering outside the confines of the crowded prison block to find wonderfully manicured and colorful gardens, and a bird rookery where elegant, snowy white egrets were nest building literally a few feet away with the Golden Gate Bridge in the background.

I do love San Francisco. My wife and I were even married under the awe-inspiring architecture of City Hall. We followed by enjoying margaritas and authentic Mexican food at Tommy's, and then rode a cable car in the cool breeze of a summer evening. A most real and unforgettable day in San Francisco!

I can honestly tell you that the spirit of San Francisco is in my bloodstream, and I cannot wait until my next visit to explore it deeper.

There are many talented photographers in the San Francisco Bay Area. I feel honored that my compilation of images taken over the last few years was selected to be published. Being from outside the city gave me a truly unbiased perspective of the city, and I took it all in with unrivaled enthusiasm and an energized attitude.

One thing is for sure, San Francisco, you will always be in my heart.

ABOVE: Cable car bells ring for a bride and groom catching a ride on Powell Street. They're among the seven million passengers who ride the cars each year.

LEFT: Wildflowers and succulents grace famously forbidding Alcatraz Island. Tended by prisoners for decades, then neglected, the gardens have been restored in recent years.

FACING PAGE: The view west from Telegraph Hill takes in two of San Francisco's most famous icons; crooked Lombard Street on neighboring Russian Hill and the Golden Gate Bridge.

LEFT: Golden Gate Park's serenely green Japanese Tea Garden dates from the Midwinter International Exposition of 1894, making it the oldest Japanese public garden in the United States. Its five soothing acres include pagodas, koi ponds and a tea house—plus plantings of cherry trees that blossom beautifully in March and April.

NEXT PAGES: Glowing in the first light of day, the Golden Gate Bridge's 1.7-mile, International Orange–painted span links San Francisco with Marin County to the north. "The mighty task is done," the bridge's engineer, Joseph P. Strauss, titled the poem he wrote to commemorate the bridge's opening in 1937. Mighty it was: the bridge took four years and $35 million (over $1 billion in today's dollars) to complete, and also cost eleven lives. Over the years it's been destroyed in numerous movies—attacked by a giant octopus in 1955's *It Came From Beneath The Sea* and swamped by a tsunami in 2015's *San Andreas*.

BELOW: Cobblestoned and garden-lined Macondray Lane ambles down the southeastern slope of Russian Hill. Its lush, slightly quirky beauty inspired Barbary Lane in Armistead Maupin's classic take on San Francisco life, *Tales of the City.*

ABOVE: At the crest of Nob Hill, the Fairmont Hotel opened in 1907, one year after its about-to-be-completed predecessor was destroyed in the San Francisco earthquake and fire. The Fairmont is rich in history—in 1945 the charter for the newly formed United Nations was drafted in its Garden Room, and guests have included numerous U.S. presidents plus Charles, the Prince of Wales.

RIGHT: The imposing, Greek Revival U.S. Mint opened on Fifth Street in 1874 to accommodate the flood of silver from Nevada's Comstock Lode. Mint operations moved to a newer building farther west in 1937, earning this structure the nickname of "the Old Mint." It's now empty, although various civic groups have proposed to turn it into a museum.

FAR RIGHT: With the Fairmont, pioneering California architect Julia Morgan, who later designed William Randolph Hearst's "castle" at San Simeon, created a Renaissance-inspired hotel meant to impress. Its lobby is dominated by Corinthian columns rising from marble floors to an ornate, gold-leaf-trimmed ceiling.

ABOVE: 1967's Summer of Love lives on in the psychedelic signage of Haight-Ashbury. Throughout much of the sixties and seventies, the neighborhood was the incense-scented capital of the American counterculture, home to rock luminaries like Janis Joplin and the Grateful Dead, and chronicled by writers like Hunter S. Thompson and Joan Didion.

LEFT TOP: San Francisco's most famous intersecting streets, Haight drew its name from a 19th-century banker while Ashbury's origins are unknown.

LEFT: Retro fashions, burritos, medical marijuana—it's all for sale on Haight Street somewhere. While neighboring blocks have gentrified, Haight itself remains indomitably scruffy, vibrant, and surprising.

FAR LEFT: Groovy on the ground floor, demure above, the Haight's Victorians and Edwardians date from the late 19th and early 20th centuries. Originally a staid, upper-middle-class neighborhood, the Haight acquired a wilder edge by the 1960s when the grand homes—many now divided up into apartments—lured hippies and hangers-on from around the world.

13

PREVIOUS PAGES: A plank pathway pointing toward the Transamerica Pyramid, a restored pier stretches into the bay from the Embarcadero waterfront. Few San Francisco neighborhoods have changed for the better as much as this one. For decades shadowed by the now-demolished Embarcadero Freeway, the water front today draws visitors for its pedestrian-friendly piers, bay views, restaurants, and attractions.

RIGHT: An antique cannon guards an entrance to the Presidio, a former fort turned national park. Founded by the Spanish in 1776 as the northernmost outpost of their New World empire, the Presidio was later taken over by Mexico and then, in 1846, by the U.S. Army. Throughout much of the 20th century it was a vital military installation. In 1994, its 1,491 acres were added to Golden Gate National Recreation Area. Today, visitors can hike its trails, splash in the San Francisco Bay at Crissy Field, dine at a number of good restaurants, and spend the night at a former army barracks turned stylish inn.

FAR RIGHT: With its Monterey cypresses and bay views, San Francisco National Cemetery ranks among the loveliest military cemeteries in the nation. Some 30,000 Americans are laid to rest here, including veterans of conflicts from the Civil War to Vietnam.

BELOW: Built in 1898, the red-brick former barracks flanking the Presidio's Main Parade Ground now house the Walt Disney Family Museum, restaurants, and offices. The large lawn is its own major attraction—popular for picnics and the weekly gathering of the Off the Grid food trucks.

ABOVE: Early morning traffic streams across the Golden Gate Bridge. While ferries and BART also carry commuters on and beneath the bay to San Francisco, the auto still rules—the bridge's average commute load is approximately 110,000 vehicle crossings per day, and a bridge fender bender can tie up U.S. Highway 101 for miles and hours.

LEFT: A freighter navigates San Francisco Bay through the early morning fog. While 19th-century San Francisco prospered as a gold rush port, the advent of giant container ships shifted most commercial shipping to the other side of the bay, in Oakland. But cruise ships and private vessels still dock in San Francisco.

RIGHT: A tangle of knotted fishing nets dangles from the Hyde Street Pier in Fisherman's Wharf. Today better known as a tourist attraction, the wharf remains an important center of commercial and sport fishing, and nearby Pier 45 houses the West Coast's largest concentration of commercial fish processors and distributors.

FAR RIGHT: Fishing boats reflect in the calm waters of Fisherman's Wharf's harbor. The earliest wharf fishing boats were lateen-rigged sailboats; these were later replaced by gas engine–powered Monterey Hull boats, many still in use today.

BELOW: It's not just human visitors who throng San Francisco's famous waterfront. On Fisherman's Wharf, Pier 39 is a popular sea lion sunning spot, too. They're substantial guests: females can reach 220 pounds, males as much as 850 pounds.

LEFT: A full moon sets behind Mission Dolores' cross, an unchanging landmark in the rapidly changing Mission District.

FAR LEFT: Ornate, twin-towered St. Ignatius Church (lit, at left of photograph) is the signature building for the University of San Francisco. For generations the Jesuit-run university has been a preferred alma mater for San Francisco politicians, businesspeople and other movers and shakers.

BELOW: Founded, in 1776, as Misión San Francisco de Asís, Mission Dolores drew its more common name from Arroyo de Los Dolores, the "Creek of Sorrows" that once ran nearby. It's composed of two churches—the simpler, original 18th-century adobe building and the more ornate adjoining basilica, completed in 1918.

With a setting overlooking San Francisco Bay, the San Francisco Giants' AT&T Park has some of the best views in the major leagues. The park's waterfront location also gives Giants the chance to go for a "splash hit"—a home run lobbed into the waters of McCovey Cove.

ABOVE: With its 245-foot tower modeled after the tower of the Seville Cathedral in Spain, the Ferry Building is a San Francisco landmark especially beloved for surviving both 1906 and 1989 earthquakes. Today it houses the restaurants and artisan food stalls of the Ferry Building Marketplace, and also an organic, locally grown Farmers Market considered to be one of the best in the nation.

RIGHT: Built for San Francisco's 1915 Panama Pacific Exposition, the Palace of Fine Arts was designed by noted California architect Bernard Maybeck to resemble a Roman ruin. Never intended to last beyond the exposition, the graceful structure became so popular among San Franciscans that they resisted all attempts to tear it down. Rebuilt as a permanent monument, it's one of the most popular sites in the city for wedding photographs.

BELOW: Perched overlooking the Golden Gate in San Francisco's northwest corner, the Palace of the Legion of Honor museum holds strong collections of European paintings and ancient art. It's also a key landmark for lovers of suspense films: fans of Alfred Hitchcock's 1958 *Vertigo* will recognize it as the museum where Kim Novak goes to visit the portrait of her grandmother, Carlotta Valdes.

LEFT: Fishnet stockings and red stilettos make a whimsical, larger-than-life Haight fashion statement.

FAR LEFT: A handsomely restored row of Queen Anne Victorians adds stately color to a neighborhood near Alamo Square. Choosing the proper shades of paint for such ornate homes is no easy feat, which is why San Francisco home color consultants do a thriving business.

BELOW: Built in 1904 as the Jefferson Hotel —which may have doubled as a brothel— The Red Victorian remains a Haight gathering spot today.

ABOVE: Glittering and lantern-decked, Grant Street is Chinatown's main thoroughfare. San Francisco's Chinatown is the oldest in the United States and, with an estimated 30,000 residents, second largest after New York's. With some 100,000 San Franciscans of Chinese ancestry, satellite Chinese neighborhoods have also grown up in the Richmond and Sunset districts on the west side of the city.

RIGHT: Lions dance during Chinatown's annual Chinese New Year's Parade, held during Lunar New Year each February. The parade is hard work: a lion costume can weigh more than 80 pounds.

FACING PAGE: Landmark meets landmark, as a cable car passes the pagoda-topped Sing Chong Building. Completed in 1908, the Sing Chong Building was the first major structure to rise in Chinatown after the 1906 earthquake and fire—and it's probably the most photographed building in Chinatown today.

RIGHT: San Francisco cuisine classics combine when crab chowder arrives in a sourdough bread bowl. Sourdough remains a San Francisco staple, with locals claiming that only the city's cool, fog-bound climate can nurture loaves of the proper tartness and texture.

FAR RIGHT: Despite its status as a tourist attraction, Fisherman's Wharf still hosts a thriving commercial fishing fleet. Sport fishing, too, is big business here, with charter boats ready to carry hopeful fishermen out for halibut, bass, and shark.

BELOW: A Fisherman's Wharf cook lifts Dungeness crabs from the steamer; the annual November opening of Dungeness crab season sparks joy throughout Northern California.

ABOVE: A marble-and-iron staircase spirals up to the Mechanics Institute Library, on Post Street in downtown San Francisco. A private lending library founded in 1854, the Mechanics Institute contains a two-story library with approximately 200,000 books, and a chess room that is home to the oldest continuously running chess club in the United States.

LEFT: An old lock guards a Cow Hollow neighborhood door mottled by rust—a common nuisance in a city surrounded on three sides by saltwater.

FAR LEFT: Downtown San Francisco glitters as glimpsed from the 40th floor of the Loews Regency Hotel. Always wary of blocking its hilly topography and views, the city has—cautiously—accepted skyscrapers as part of its tech-fueled boom, with many of the newest towers rising in the South of Market neighborhood.

ABOVE: The Mission District has been a center for public art, particularly murals, for half a century. Its Balmy Alley holds the city's most concentrated collection of murals, many of them with political themes—like O'Brien Thiele and Miranda Bergman's rainbow-wrapped *The Culture Contains the Seed of Resistance.*

RIGHT: Another notable Balmy Alley mural is Edythe Boone's *Those We Love, We Remember,* which pays powerful tribute to loved ones lost.

FACING PAGE: San Francisco's 21st-century rise as a wealthy tech center has brought numerous changes to the Mission District and other neighborhoods. In Balmy Alley, Tirzo Araiza and Lucia Ippolito's *Mission Makeover* depicts the conflicts generated as the mostly working-class Mission gentrifies.

FAR LEFT: Experience the life aquatic at Aquarium of the Bay's see-through underwater tunnels. On Pier 39, the aquarium houses 20,000 bay and Pacific creatures, from octopuses to sharks.

LEFT: The most endangered wolf species in the world, the Mexican gray wolf is star of the show at the San Francisco Zoo and Gardens' Wolf Canyon exhibit.*

BELOW: Mom and baby reticulated giraffe nuzzle at the San Francisco Zoo and Gardens. The zoo is home to 1,000 endangered and rescued animals. It also houses the Little Puffer Miniature Steam Train, beloved by generations of San Francisco children.*

SAN FRANCISCO ZOO PHOTOS COURTESY OF MARIANNE HALE AND THE SAN FRANCISCO ZOO AND GARDENS

RIGHT: The Golden Gate Bridge rises above Fort Point. Called "The Gibraltar of the Pacific," the brick-and-mortar fortress was completed in 1861 to protect San Francisco Bay (and the California goldfields) from foreign attack. During the Civil War, as many as 500 Union soldiers were garrisoned here.

BELOW: Wet-suited against the 56-degree water, a solo surfer catches a wave beneath the Golden Gate Bridge. As noted author and surfer William Finnegan puts it: "Hypothermia is, indeed, the greatest single hazard of surfing in San Francisco."

LEFT: In the Mission District, Dolores Park offers mostly reliable sun in a frequently fog-bound city. That makes it one of San Francisco's most popular spots to picnic or spread out a beach towel and improve your tan.

FAR LEFT: Aquatic Park's lawns and trees provide a welcome green space just a short walk from Fisherman's Wharf and the San Francisco Maritime National Historic Park.

BELOW: Alta Plaza Park boasts a fine playground, expansive views, and a location in one of the city's richest neighborhoods, Pacific Heights. Surrounding homes go for tens of millions of dollars—but the playground is, thankfully, free.

ABOVE: Where North Beach flows into the Financial District, one triangular icon meets another, as the 48-story Transamerica Pyramid, built in 1972, rises behind the flatiron-shaped Sentinel Building. The latter was built in 1905 and later restored by director Francis Ford Coppola.

RIGHT: Vintage streetcars of SF MUNI's F Line roll through Fisherman's Wharf. Nearly as historic as the more famous cable cars, the 1920s-vintage F Line streetcars were brought in from Philadelphia and Milan, Italy; they run along the waterfront and up and down Market Street.

ABOVE: Looking east from the Marin Headlands, the Golden Gate Bridge stands silhouetted against the waters of San Francisco Bay. Covering 550 square miles, the bay is by far the largest estuary on the West Coast.

LEFT: Sunrise lights San Francisco Bay as seen from Hawk Hill, in the Marin Headlands just north of the Golden Gate Bridge. Part of Golden Gate National Recreation Area, the hill is famous for its views and—as the name suggests—its annual autumn raptor migration.

LEFT: Alcatraz Cruises' *Islander* begins its voyage to "The Rock." Each year, 1.3 million people visit the former prison, thrilling to the tales of hardened criminals and enjoying the spectacular island views.

FACING PAGE: The last standing guard tower rises above the Alcatraz Island dock. Established as a U.S. Army fort in the 1850s, the island served as a federal penitentiary from 1934 to 1963. The surrounding bay's chill waters and strong currents discouraged escape. But they're not really unswimmable, as participants in the annual Escape from Alcatraz 1.5-mile Triathlon swim can testify.

BELOW: Corridor "Broadway" separates Alcatraz cell blocks B and C. The prison was intended to be a "super prison," designed to eliminate all possible communication between prisoners and the outside world. Among the approximately 1,500 criminals imprisoned here over Alcatraz' 50-year life as a penitentiary were gang leader Al Capone and "The Birdman of Alcatraz," murderer-turned-amateur-ornithologist Robert Stroud.

BROADWAY

RIGHT: Near Fisherman's Wharf, the Powell-Hyde cable car rattles past The Buena Vista Café—said to be the birthplace of Irish coffee.

FAR RIGHT: The ornate Phelan Building (built in 1908 by James D. Phelan, one of the city's most respected mayors) rises above Market Street. Starting at the Embarcadero and extending through the Castro District to the southwest, Market Street serves as San Francisco's Main Street, ranging from glamorous to gritty to middle-class along its five-mile path.

BELOW: The grande dame of Union Square, the Westin St. Francis Hotel opened in 1902, was nearly destroyed in the 1906 earthquake and fire, but rebuilt and reopened the following year. The glass elevator ride up its 32-floor Pacific Tower gives some of the most dizzying views in the city.

ABOVE: A California Street cable car makes the steep descent toward Market Street, the Bay Bridge glimpsed behind it. There are currently forty-four cable cars in operation, and while the system is historic the cars are not—new ones are manufactured in a small factory in the city's Dogpatch neighborhood.

LEFT: Claes Oldenburg and Coosje van Bruggen's *Cupid's Span* adds a note of whimsical romance to the Embarcadero waterfront, with the Ferry Building's tower behind it. Dismantling the Embarcadero Freeway—damaged beyond repair in the 1989 Loma Prieta earthquake—let the waterfront blossom with gardens and public art.

53

ABOVE: Founded in 1776 and completed in 1791, Mission Dolores is the oldest building in San Francisco. Some 26,000 adobe bricks were used to erect its four-foot-thick walls.

TOP RIGHT: A few blocks west of Union Square, Glide Memorial Church is famous for its gospel choir and its decades-long tradition of social activism, including a Daily Free Meals Program that serves up to 2,400 meals per day.

RIGHT: The soaring interior of St. Mary's Cathedral evokes heaven and the earthly world that surrounds the church.

FACING PAGE: Twin-towered Saints Peter and Paul Catholic Church has been a center of the North Beach neighborhood since 1912. Begun as a church for North Beach's large Italian community, it now conducts services in English and Cantonese, too.

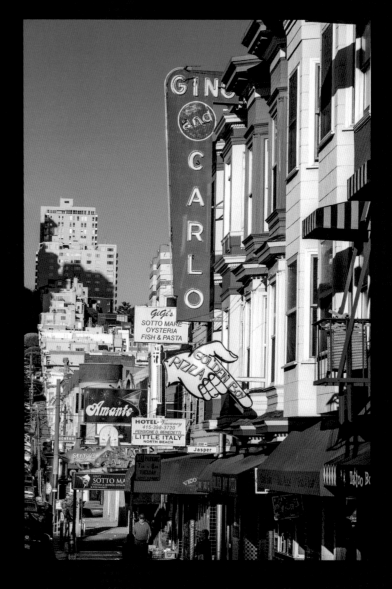

ABOVE: Busy Green Street leads through the heart of proudly Italian North Beach. The neighborhood began attracting Italian immigrants in the late 1800s, and while it's not as solidly Italian as it was in decades past, it remains the city's most authentically atmospheric place to order some spaghetti carbonara and a glass of good red wine.

LEFT: A 19th century chocolate factory, Ghirardelli Square, not far from Fisherman's Wharf, became one of the United States' earliest and most successful examples of repurposing vintage industrial buildings into shopping and dining centers. With dozens of shops and restaurants, it remains a prime visitor destination today.

RIGHT: One of San Francisco's loveliest secret stairways, the Filbert Steps climb—and climb and climb—Telegraph Hill from Sansome Street up to Coit Tower. As you climb the steps, listen for the famous "Wild Parrots of Telegraph Hill."

FAR RIGHT: A peaceful respite from the busy city, the green, misty, fern-carpeted coast redwood groves of Marin County's Muir Woods National Monument contains trees that rise 250 feet tall. Scientifically dubbed *Sequoia sempervirens* ("ever-living" for their up-to-2,000-years lifespan), coast redwoods are found only in a narrow band along the Pacific from southwest Oregon to Big Sur, California.

BELOW: Stairs ascend Russian Hill Park—a leafy refuge on a densely populated hill. The hill's name is said to have originated from seven Cyrillic-inscribed gravestones found at the top of the hill. One story tells that the graves are from a boatload of Russian sailors who died while docked in San Francisco in the early 1800s.

LEFT: Rainbow crosswalks celebrate the Castro District's place as the center of San Francisco's gay community. The city has the highest percentage of LGBT (lesbian, gay, bisexual, and transgender) residents in the nation.

FACING PAGE: No dinky multiplex: with its Spanish Baroque architecture, giant screen, and mighty Wurlitzer organ, the 1922-vintage Castro Theater makes moviegoing an event. San Francisco film fans applaud it for its showing of classic movies, plus special events like its *Sound of Music* sing-along.

NEXT PAGES: Racing yachts speed past Alcatraz for the America's Cup competition. Stiff winds and tricky currents make San Francisco Bay sailing challenging even for experts.

BELOW: A historic Market F Line streetcar navigates the Castro and Market Street turnaround. Behind and just to the right of it is Twin Peaks Tavern, one of San Francisco's longest-established gay bars.

LEFT: North Beach hangout Vesuvio Café beckons where Columbus Avenue meets Jack Kerouac Alley. Beat-era novelist Kerouac didn't live in San Francisco for long—only a few months, in fact—but his hard-drinking, nonconformist spirit still imbues this part of town.

BELOW: Sheltered (usually) from San Francisco's wind and fog, the Marina District is one of the city's safer bets for outdoor dining. The neighborhood is also known for attracting stylish legions of recent Stanford and Cal (and other college) grads to its bars, restaurants, and boutiques.

ABOVE: The Murphy Windmill stands at the far western edge of Golden Gate Park, not far from its older brother, the Dutch Windmill. When built in the early 1900s, both pumped water that was used to irrigate the park. Today, they are merely ornamental but make terrific backdrops for smartphone photos.

RIGHT: A splashing fountain makes its own melody at Golden Gate Park's Music Concourse. Set between the de Young Museum and the California Academy of Sciences, the concourse is home to weekend band concerts and everyday picnicking.

ABOVE: Sculpture depicts Japanese life in California in the early 20th century. Prior to World War II, San Francisco's thirty-block Japantown was one of the biggest in the nation. Today, a more compact neighborhood is dominated by the Japan Center mall and shops and restaurants on nearby Post Street.

LEFT: Tokyo comes to San Francisco in the Japan Center mall, where you can buy Japanese antiques and hardware, and eat sushi, soba noodles, or steak.

FACING PAGE: The green-tile-roofed Dragon Gate marks the Bush Street entrance to Chinatown. Adorned by sculptures of dragons, fish, and lions, it's based on the ceremonial gates—*paifang*—found in Chinese villages.

ABOVE: The Exploratorium, on Pier 15 on the Embarcadero, is widely acclaimed as one of the most innovative (and fun) science museums in the world. Want to learn about sound, light, electricity, and gravity—and get unbeatable bay views? You will here.

RIGHT: Howard Street traffic zips past Moscone Convention Center in SOMA—South of Market. Formerly a faded industrial district, the new SOMA's hotels and restaurants—and cultural must-sees like the San Francisco Museum of Modern Art—draw business travelers, vacationers, and locals.

CF 5597 AJ

A Perilous
Entrance

THE GOLDEN GATE
Powerful tides and gale-force
winds sweep through this
narrow and rocky opening,
a dangerous place often
hidden by fog.

LEFT: San Francisco's life as a major Pacific port is celebrated at San Francisco Maritime National Historic Park, on the bay just west of Fisherman's Wharf. Ships by the hundreds carried gold-seekers to San Francisco during the gold rush—as many as 62,000 between the spring of 1849 and 1850 alone, all making the treacherous sea voyage around South America's Cape Horn to California.

BELOW: Fish ahoy! Founded by a branch of the Alioto family who first emigrated to San Francisco from Sicily in 1898, Capurro's restaurant has been serving cioppino and Dungeness crab on Fisherman's Wharf since the 1940s.

RIGHT: From the 210-foot-top of Coit Tower, Bay Area views extend in all directions—from this window, looking across San Francisco to the northwest.

FAR RIGHT: Lillie Hitchcock Coit never saw the tower that she paid for and that bears her name: it was completed in 1933, four years after her death. Famed San Francisco newspaperman Herb Caen called the white, art deco tower—visible from much of the city—"very much an exclamation point at the end of an unfinished sentence."

BELOW: Legend says Lillie Hitchcock Coit, the wealthy eccentric who commissioned the tower, had it designed to resemble a hose nozzle in honor of San Francisco's volunteer firemen. That's not true—but Coit did commission a firemen's monument in nearby Washington Square.

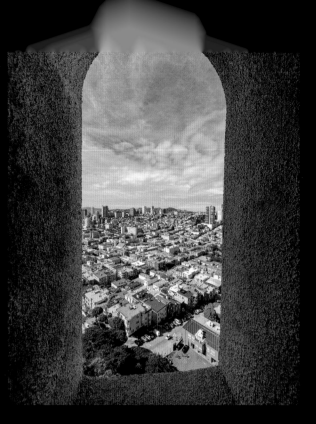

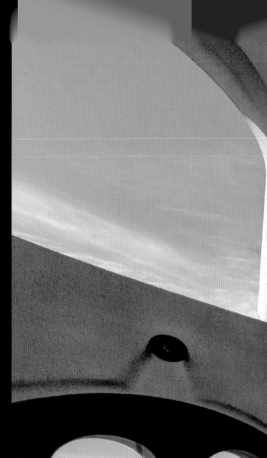

ABOVE: This purple and gold paint job shows wh[y]
Victorians are frequently referred to as "Painted L[adies.]
the city like its historic houses so bright? One ex[planation]
sultant Bob Buckter—aka "Dr. Color," who has a[dvised on]
colors for thousands of San Francisco Victoria[ns, is the]
influence of the psychedelic 1960s.

LEFT: Possibly the most photographed houses [in the city, the]
Steiner Street Victorians across from Alamo Squ[are date from]
the 1890s. They're featured on countless postca[rds and views]
of San Francisco; TV fans will recognize them fr[om the opening]
sequence of the long-running sitcom, *Full House.*

ABOVE: *Winged Victory* poses atop the Dewey Monument in Union Square. The 1903 monument honors Admiral George Dewey's victories in the Philippines during the Spanish-American War in 1898.

RIGHT: Quiet at dawn, Union Square will soon bustle with shoppers, businesspeople, and visitors from around the world. The 2.6-acre square functions as downtown's patio and recreation room, home to art exhibits, concerts, and, during the holiday season, an ice rink.

ABOVE: The intricate, elegant ceiling of the San Francisco City Hall rotunda features four medallions by the famous sculptor Henri Crenier.

RIGHT: City Hall was built to replace an equally imposing structure destroyed in the 1906 earthquake. Two blocks big, it's considered one of the finest examples of Beaux Arts architecture in the country—a suitably imposing seat of government for a city that, despite its relatively small population (about 860,000), thinks of itself as one of the most important in the world.

FACING PAGE, TOP LEFT: The Ceremonial Rotunda is a favored spot for San Francisco weddings. Among the celebrities hitched in the building were baseball legend Joe DiMaggio and his beautiful bride, Marilyn Monroe.

FACING PAGE, TOP RIGHT: Covered with 23.5 carat gold leaf, it is the tallest dome in the United States—at 307 feet 6 inches, 42 feet higher than the United States Capitol dome in Washington, D.C.

FACING PAGE, BOTTOM: The rotunda features Tennessee pink marble floors, Colorado limestone walls. and a grand staircase that leads to the Ceremonial Rotunda.

ABOVE: The marquee for the Metro Theater (now a gym) welcomes you to Union Street in the Cow Hollow neighborhood. Wedged between the Marina and Pacific Heights, Cow Hollow is one of the city's most popular shopping and dining districts.

RIGHT: Founded by poet Lawrence Ferlinghetti in 1953, City Lights Bookstore still shines a powerful literary light on North Beach today. Want a current best seller? It will be here. But so will obscure, wonderful books by writers you may have never heard of.

PREVIOUS PAGES: Long, lonely, windswept Ocean Beach forms the city's western boundary, stretching from Land's End in the city's northwest corner to Fort Funston at the city's southwest. Stiff breezes make it a tempting venue for expert kite surfers who brave the cold water and powerful surf.

ABOVE: Cyclists make their morning commute down Market Street, following "The Wiggle," the known-to-the-cognoscenti bike route that minimizes hill climbs. In a crowded city, cyclists have to compete with pedestrians and autos for street space. Groups like the San Francisco Bicycle Coalition are working to make San Francisco more bike-friendly.

LEFT: Rush hour packs this BART station. The Bay Area Rapid Transit system carries approximately 421,000 riders each weekday, linking San Francisco to the East Bay and Northern Peninsula.

FAR LEFT: A Powell-Hyde line cable car rotates on the turntable near Aquatic Park. Inventor Andrew Smith Hallidie was inspired to devise the cable railway after seeing horses struggling to haul cars up one of the city's steep hills.

ABOVE: A cascading waterfall graces the Martin Luther King Memorial at Yerba Buena Gardens in the South of Market neighborhood. The two-block park also contains a children's museum and carousel, the excellent Yerba Buena Center for the Arts, and an expansive lawn good for picnicking.

RIGHT: The *San Francisco Belle* paddleboat docks on the Embarcadero. The water-front is busy with boats today but—amazingly—a number of 19th-century vessels lie buried beneath the ground here and in the nearby Financial District, scuttled then paved over and built upon.

LEFT: Sailboats dock in Marin County's Sausalito and behind it, glide past Angel Island, the largest natural island in San Francisco Bay. Now a state park, the island served for decades as the West Coast's Ellis Island, processing tens of thousands of immigrants, most from China.

NEXT PAGES: A San Francisco sunset casts a glow over the Golden Gate Bridge and Russian Hill, where headlights outline the famous zigzags of Lombard Street.

BELOW: One of the most-visited historic ships in the country, the square-rigger *Balclutha* docks at Hyde Street Pier in San Francisco Maritime Historic National Park. The ship made its first 140-day voyage from Wales to California in 1887, bringing coal and returning with California wheat. Later, it was used to carry lumber between the Pacific Northwest and Australia.

ABOVE: The California Academy of Science's undulating living roof is lush with 1.7 million plants that provide habitat for birds, bees and butterflies. Located in Golden Gate Park, across from the de Young Museum, the Academy contains the Morrison Planetarium, Steinhart Aquarium, and the Osher Rainforest, a four-story dome whose dense vegetation and tropical animals make visitors feel like they've entered the Amazon.

LEFT: Anchoring the east side of the Civic Center, the Asian Art Museum is one of the best in the nation, containing 18,000 works from China, Japan, Korea, and other Asian nations. Its Café Asia is a fine spot to enjoy a Hong Kong noodle salad or sip Silk Road tea.

FACING PAGE: The stately San Francisco Opera House reflects a city crazy about classical music—both the opera and the San Francisco Symphony earn accolades worldwide. Opera and symphony opening nights are among the city's most glittering social events, with music patrons decked out in tuxedos and evening gowns, hoping to be featured in the *San Francisco Chronicle* social pages the following day.

ABOVE: Popular among runners who want to test their lungs and leg muscles, the Lyon Street Steps runs along the west side of Pacific Heights. The tiny neighborhood commands some of the city's best views—and highest real estate prices.

RIGHT: Looking north from the top of Coit Tower, you gaze down on the Embarcadero and Fisherman's Wharf, and out to Angel Island and Marin County.

PREVIOUS PAGES: Twin Peaks' glittering nighttime view stretches from the Golden Gate Bridge to downtown and beyond. At 922 feet, the city-owned peak is the second-highest point in San Francisco—the less auto-accessible, 928-foot Mount Davidson is number one.

ABOVE: A Powell Street cable car pauses for passengers. Two lines—Powell-Mason and Powell-Hyde—begin where Powell meets Market Street.

LEFT: Powell Street climbs Nob Hill from Union Square. The Sears Fine Food's sign trumpets a San Francisco restaurant serving comfort food—think meat loaf, pot roast, and, above all, Swedish pancakes—since 1938.

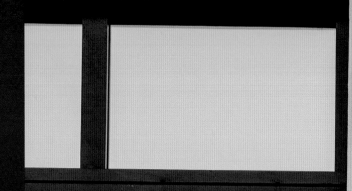

ABOVE: Built in 1898, the Ferry Building still greets thousands of ferry commuters daily, traveling in from Marin County and Oakland and Alameda in the East Bay. It also brings together Northern California's best artisan food producers—of olive oil, bread, cheese, coffee, produce, wine, and more—under one elegantly arching roof.

RIGHT: The Bay Bridge reflection floats in the waterfront windows of the Epic Steak restaurant, on the Embarcadero.

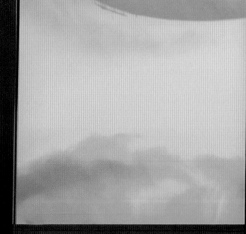

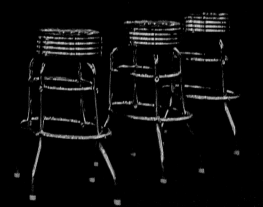

ABOVE: The Poky LaFarge Band takes the stage at The Fillmore. Opened as a dance hall in 1912, The Fillmore became the most famous rock venue in the world in the 1960s and 70s, hosting legends and future legends from the Grateful Dead to Aretha Franklin to Tom Petty.

LEFT: Posters from rock concerts past decorate The Fillmore's bar area, where a local musician tunes up before his turn on stage. Musicians who got their start here include Jefferson Airplane and Santana; current performers range from Willie Nelson to Wilco.

ABOVE: From prison to nature preserve: snowy white egrets nest on formerly forbidding Alcatraz Island, with the Golden Gate Bridge stretching behind them.

RIGHT: A whale breeches in San Francisco Bay, with Alcatraz Island in the background. Stricter environmental regulations over the past twenty years has made the bay noticeably cleaner and more friendly to marine life, including whales and sharks.

FAR RIGHT: A steep hike from Land's End leads to the ruins of Sutro Baths. Built by millionaire mining engineer Adolph Sutro, the baths drew San Franciscans by the tens of thousands when they opened in 1894. The business later failed and burned to the ground; today the ruins are a picturesque part of Golden Gate National Recreation Area.

ABOVE: The heart of downtown San Francisco, Union Square glows with an appropriately romantic piece of public art—one of the "Hearts in San Francisco" sculptures created by artists and placed around the city annually to raise money for charity.

LEFT: Looking down at the "City by the Bay" from Russian Hill, Broadway cuts east past Chinatown and then through neon-signed North Beach to the Embarcadero waterfront, with the Bay Bridge shining behind it.

RIGHT: The Cliff House perches on an overlook above Land's End and the Pacific. Popular for its cocktails and ocean views, the current Cliff House is the direct descendent of a restaurant built here in 1863; back then diners had to arrive by horse and carriage after an arduous seven-mile journey from downtown San Francisco.

FAR RIGHT: Part of Golden Gate National Recreation Area, Land's End, on the city's northwestern corner overlooking the Golden Gate, is rich in views, trails, and hidden beaches.

BELOW: Fishing village turned tourist hub, Marin County's Sausalito is a cyclist's paradise. Ambitious riders can even pedal across the Golden Gate Bridge for a Sausalito lunch stop, then pedal back; the less ambitious can just rent bikes in town.

ABOVE: A cable car rolls along Mason Street, passing white-spired Nuestra Señora de Guadalupe Catholic Church. Built in 1912, it replaced an earlier structure destroyed in the 1906 earthquake and was for decades a center of San Francisco's Mexican American community.

LEFT: The Cable Car Museum on Mason Street salutes the invented-in-San Francisco public transit wonders. Nearly shut down in the 1950s, the cable cars were saved by popular demand and designated the United States' first moving National Historic Landmark in the 1960s.

ABOVE: Sunset silhouettes a stickball game in Alamo Square Park. The park has venerable roots—it dates all the way back to 1856.

RIGHT: The sun's last rays light the Marin headlands and the Golden Gate Bridge. The glorious gap between Marin County and the city of San Francisco got its name in 1846 from explorer John C. Fremont, who compared it to the "Golden Horn," the harbor of ancient Byzantium, now Istanbul.

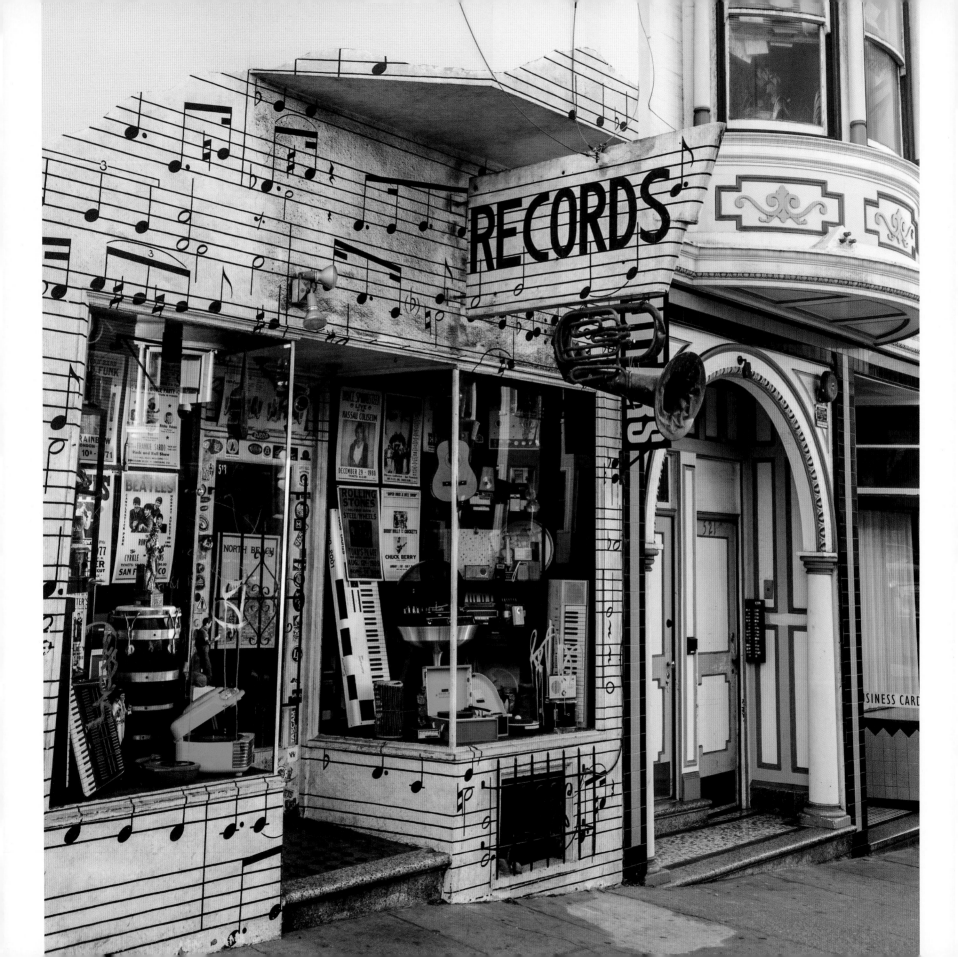

ABOVE: A "Hearts in San Francisco" sculpture marks the start of an only-in-San Francisco cardio workout—the Lyon Street steps, which climb from Cow Hollow to Pacific Heights. The two flights of sixty-two steps each are so challenging that they're wildly popular among the city's personal trainers.

LEFT: A rainbow of drying laundry hangs from a Chinatown fire escape. Most of the crowded neighborhood's buildings date from immediately after the 1906 earthquake.

FACING PAGE: In a city whose economy is increasingly dominated by tech, venture capital, and social media, some traditions live on—like turntables and vinyl LPs at this North Beach music store.

BELOW: Farmers and factory workers populate the murals inside Coit Tower, along with San Franciscans playing tennis, reading newspapers, and crowding the city's sidewalks. Beloved today, the murals were highly controversial when they were painted in 1934, with critics claiming some artists displayed Communist leanings.

ABOVE: Broadway Tunnel slices beneath Russian Hill. Opened in 1952, it provides speedier access between Chinatown and Van Ness Avenue to the west.

RIGHT: The view from the Loews Regency Hotel's 40th floor shows the Transamerica Pyramid. At 853 feet, it is still the tallest building in San Francisco, and was controversial when it was built in 1972, with critics claiming the triangular design was awkward. Today it's accepted and, at least among many San Franciscans, loved. Behind it shines Coit Tower, Russian Hill, and San Francisco Bay.

NEXT PAGE: The Bay Bridge's car-lit western span makes a golden pathway from Yerba Buena Island to San Francisco. Opened in 1936, the bridge is actually a year older than the more famous Golden Gate, and more heavily used, with approximately 240,000 vehicle crossings per day.